Companions, Analogies

Brian Swann

Companions, Analogies

Brian Swann

Sheep Meadow Press
Rhinebeck, New York

Designed and typeset by The Sheep Meadow Press
Distributed by The University Press of New England

Cover image: Matisse, *Nuit de Noel* 1952 (maquette)
Author photo: Marget Long

Library of Congress Cataloging-in-Publication Data

Names: Swann, Brian, author.
Title: Companions, analogies / Brian Swann.
Description: Rhinebeck, NY : Sheep Meadow Press, 2016. | Includes
   bibliographical references.
Identifiers: LCCN 2016012576 | ISBN 9781937679668
Classification: LCC PS3569.W256 A6 2016 | DDC 811/.54--dc23
LC record available at https://lccn.loc.gov/2016012576

All inquiries and permission requests should be addressed to the publisher:

The Sheep Meadow Press
PO Box 84
Rhinebeck, NY 12514

For Roberta, as always, forever, with love

Contents

Part One

(i)

DE SENECTUTE OR BEST YOU CAN

I have nothing more to go on, not even
   that—a half of something, a half-life, less
and something else, and wonder if this would
   be enough for another life, in another life,
and if what was had the compatibility to
   suck on time, suck in time, help me live
in it if only in the way of my recurrent
   nightmare of still living in the house I sold
years ago, prowling about, anxious, on the alert,
   like the priest at Nemi, until time continued
with the silent crush of whatever it's made of
   that from a distance looks like a still flower,
red and white, or just white, or red, coming
   at you balancing on "itself", which is what
I'll call what it's in, something like a brilliant
   hummingbird flying forward backwards so
fast you can't see it, or a bubble balanced on
   a meniscus so you can't see it but it makes you
think of what comes next in another time when
   nothing does, so how do you talk about something
like eternity without using grammar which is
   shape, sequence, number, without needing
a mask to pull on helping you pretend you
   exist even if somewhere else since once
you've put it on you've lost sight of it and don't
   know who it says you're supposed to be and
have no basis for action, or otherwise, and could
   do anything and nothing could be proved against
you, then as you leave everything behind and have
   no idea what all this would be in another life
or lives let alone this, when we live on without
   knowing, perhaps next to, in front, behind, on top,
beneath everything and nothing, and whatever is
   between everything else, the way we don't look

at just one thing but relations between ourselves
   and things, which means what we see is always
floating in the gaps on the way to be something else,
   elsewhere, even "yourself" or whatever you go by now ,
or with whatever there is left to judge with and which
   you hope enough to get on, best you can.

HEADING OUT

Behind curtains drawn across cobbled back lanes, in the parlor kept for show,
a table and chairs, untouched harmonium, curiosity cabinet, a fire only shadows

on a screen, caged bird a penny played. Here a boy, standing on the table, reaches
past the gold-leaf frame, through a forest of giant trees to slide his fingers

down the only beam of light to a dark pool where on a rock a naked man looks up,
head back, mouth open, calling the way a stone might, his voice rising to the boy

the way waves rise, shaking off the cries of gulls while across the parlor wall
five ceramic ducks fly in formation, each smaller than the one in front, heading

through the window and out across the lane, across continents, to where they
don't know, or when there won't know if they're there, or here, or somewhere else.

QUANTUM FOR BREAKFAST

You're sitting at the table, which they used to say was empty, but now
the table's waking too, flying about opening hallways and entryways, corridors
and staircases, whole families crammed into what used to be porticoes, camped
under campaniles, stuck under stones, under aqueducts, and if they choose

their particles can fly around at breakneck speed like hummingbirds in
Teotihuacan or pass through someone sitting on a barstool in Trastevere,
or even you about to jump off a roof holding pillows in front while wondering
if fractals have fractals and if so how long and how far and how many worlds

are there and for how long, for as Alcmaeon said aeons ago, man dies because
he cannot join his end to his beginning, and some other sage said there are worlds
extending in every direction, visible and invisible, so we do not live in this
little moment but in that world extending in every direction, and Plato himself

said mind resides in seeing affinities simultaneously, and Ibnul Arabi that there is
no such thing as time, and someone else claimed that the non-existence of the world
was never in *time*, so I sit half-asleep with this still in my head waiting for what's
in store from a world not what it is, waiting for what it might be.

THE THRUSH

Time's shining echoes, rivers on which
we drift downstream, floating over
drowned towns whose voices rise

and flow around rocks, figures in smoke,
shadows of the shadowless, and when
looking up there are trees, or trees up trees,

expressing sky with migrating birds, until
the pole-star's mill-beam turns, grinding
from eternity time in which a year's

a month, a month a day, a day an hour, an hour
even less but with enough for me to listen
to the hermit thrush who each day prays the sun up

out of the ground, floating it over the rough wall
where I wait, listening, in air staunch as stone
that opens flowers of the trumpet-vine, here

where the mind reaches out as time drifts in
the rhythm of light fragrant as hyssop,
luminous as air, beyond itself.

THE WAY

thrush song flows over the stone wall
arriving the way each star comes when I call,

the way I make the stream dance up and down
the hill when I watch, slick as an eel, the way

that web on the twig flinches in a puff of light
when I look, the way dawn creaks, grows

so slow I feel I could wring light out faster myself,
the way clouds float by and stones stretch so far

I can't fix their shadows until they hold their breath
then, time to let go, curl round and sleep as

the land darkens, heaves up into the distance
called mountains, purple as gentians, where

dark figures are moving off, the way the eye shakes
and flickers as it fixes a world you can touch.

MORE

Last night in a dream I traced the edges of leaves,
stems and blossoms with a Micron 02 pen on top

of a sheet like Plexiglas which hadn't yet been
invented. Pressing hard on a top flat and secure as

a sheet of paper, I concentrated to get each curl and
edge right, before standing back to admire my work.

That was when I noticed more to it than surface. Lifting
the box against the light, plants glowed inside, fixed

at the height of their growing season, floating immutable
as if in ether, in more than four dimensions. I tried to get

closer, inside without opening, catch each niche and
nuance, fleck and fragrance, trace it on itself without

changing a thing but making it mine, or at least more
than itself, more than me, more than its finale.

OFF-BEAT

At dawn the street shines bright enough to rest your back on.
Soon a car door slams and more chime in in ways you know by now,

one by one. An alarm goes off, setting others off. A bar of light
cracks the pane. Then wind frees hard-edged leaves so they flail

against the glass like stuff that flies through dream. I can't go out.
I stay inside, speak quietly to myself, one flake at a time floating

down in an off-beat, dry before it can stain the stone it lands on.

PALIMPSEST

Sky unravels into flames, spits
and slips off, leaving its after-image,

palimpsest of an ancient map that
still populates us with monsters,

still draws us in to see what's no
longer there.

                   *

        Lights in the storm-tossed
house flicker on and off, phone dead,

shelves shake, shelves shake, a child
screams, someone's in the rafters, time-

slip tourists we'll take to the moon,
stars if we reach them.

                   *

           Gods
you can't unthink are the clatter

of pebbles in a stream, eternity's
rushing void, voice of the scuppernong

and whisper of the Pleiades, the rustle
of their plumage is frost's trace catching

on twigs, snow catching night sky,
spreading it over the pasture,

while in the mirror, someone rises
out of me and then someone

13

else and then another out of her and
another out of him, and I wake deep

in the mirror, shadowing myself.

WHO OF SHADOW

Shadows have shadows. Sometimes
that's all they are, all the way

down. They can broaden you out,
tighten you up, run as fast, stay as still,

move without you, without moving you.
When you look down you can trace

their nothing but can't see them
sideways. They refigure light as dark

but won't break down, just drift away,
adjust to what you still can't get, you

who breathe shadows elusive as owls:
Who? Who? Who do you think you are?

THE LEAST OF IT

We lose nothing by not knowing since
everything is ours and we give it away
freely. It may fit perfectly, but now it's

too late I want it back, this is not a one-
way street or mirror, you can't wear me
like a hat, one size does not fit all though

I still plead for you to make room, the way
the moon does or, presumably, the sun
though it's too far away to know for sure,

and I am at the point of my life when I
realize we are not trees, never were, nor birds
or mountains, not anything we can't be,

the unseen is still the unseen, or if it's
seen is meaningless as shadows, for what
might have been no longer is and that

leaves us with very little, just deserts and
formulae for more of what we already are
but no plans for anything else, or more, which

is what we really need, and now it's too late
to be as we reach for fire that won't burn but
with no way to hold it or put it out once it's

eaten our hands, the pool and all the genes now
gutted, just this side of nothing, everything
flapping, and that, as I said, is the least of it.

FIRE WITH FIRE

overwhelming, wings catching, a taste for everything, hammers
striking sparks, reaching, its flowers roar and spit scattering scraps—oh, there, how
the hawk tilts over and away, loses itself as I hide and peer through the conflagration

taller than trees it takes out to see roads petering away where the twister hit, lightning
caught and way off burned-out sky in its poverty, its ashen aftermath, until the wheel
turns to night I breathe over the lake now clear with new heavens, smoke-wisps

cooled to unearthly lights, flickering liquid all round me in flames, swimming sky-water,
water-sky, bird entering unknown shapes and shadows, nebulous, how glorious
in amorphous echoes of skeins and flares that flutter around me viridian, amethyst,

streaks roseate and mauve, watered saffron and shot silk filtering air while an owl calls,
coyotes sing, dip and quiver, night winds calling soft flames, new fire staining my skin
as I float on my back, sky flowing through my fingers, in my mouth.

BECOMING

The beat of oars, precise footprints neat as shadows over
the surface of the void, moving together, race along the course

with no room for the approximate, leaving a trail to follow
the way letters began as the mark of cranes, messages in the blue,

and where to go forward you look back at the irreversible,
the consequence, chaining you to it, its tight whorls moving over

the surface, so it's as if you stay and they move, telling a story
in which you can't see where you're going until you've been there,

become what you are and betray at your peril.

ABSORBED

The sea glitters piecemeal, scatters, seeking an exit from
its surface, driving down where cannot be seen, pinions

of thrust, grab, wide open, writhing walls of force neither
inside nor out, heavy as held breath, light as breath suspended,

bulked with all the creatures in it, calling in cadences of distance,
the thrum of desire, and I want to follow, trying to find something

not there, find a space where space hasn't been discovered, where
there is no need to know the name of where you are, for when you

do know you are no longer there but in what you've made and from
this there's no escape, it has absorbed you. But I've tried too hard

and instead listen offshore where a glacier pours into the ocean
muffled bells, watch stinging salt shatter into cloud tatter, absorbed.

AT THE OPERA

"*die Scenerie war Abschied*"
—Rilke, "The Fourth Elegy"

If you look out to sea, you see what the sea wants,
but here it is painted backdrop behind the sailing ship
on wheels that's pulled along by ropes behind the balustrade
till it has to stop and disappear as marionettes, moving
with jerky emotions, sing their farewell duet, the sea
unmoving, waves' skin stretched and gleaming over
an invisible shoal. But we will cut the sea some slack,
puppets too, who are doing as well as can be expected,
and as for the music, it is almost too big to hear as it
evokes absence, opens up loneliness for which there
can be no preparation since it always comes on its
own terms, even via dolls. So I close my eyes. Too late.
The seas have risen, a gale in the rigging is tearing the
sheets apart, snapping ropes and stays, until a wave
washes the crew overboard, wrecks the ship on the shoal.
The curtain falls. The sea rolls up. Puppets crumple.
Who's there?

HIGH-TIDE MARK

Such ordinary moments, unsorted evenings
like those which by tomorrow
will be evenings again like these
staring from back of the mirror,
foreshortened, blank, wide as paper,
their eyes on me before I even looked
to see if I could pass through their doors
into a place all windowed, looked at
by my own reflections, complete coherence
where there is none, no fore or hindsight,
complete in the prayer of the other,
unfiltered until floating shapeless
and in place there's the taste
of light, crystalline, perfumed as sky
going on for ever, a place where I could
patch the porch once and for all,
install a water pump, find a way to keep
the roof on and damp out, a place where
the five ordinary senses become exceptional
as they float in the glass, keeping it honest,
the way the desert blooms, yellow and frothy,
musical as a beach where the tide comes in,
goes out, leaving oranges I once found
shiny as glass at the high-tide mark.

WIND

No leftovers, no bygones, no tuning fork,
it fits everything everywhere, obstructions

only diversions, filling the incomplete,
expanding the excessive, excessive as desire,

raising the useless, staking everything on itself,
no hedging, resolving the unseen,

shaking shadows, driving the discarded,
uprooting whys, whats and wherefores

resolving the various, evidenced in its effect,
known by results, the unseen hand.

FALLING

As the stream suddenly spills from quarried-
out heights, rises and snags on itself, chokes

in spray, balanced in its back flow, freighted
with rocks, stones, trees, star-shards, crushing

itself with its own weight, a leaf caught in
an updraft is tossed about, falling but steadied

by its own shape, free as it falls so as I watch
I say it is almost not falling at all, it is hardly

a leaf as it opens a space for itself, tracing
emptiness etching itself on air.

TO BE TREE

"*O hoher Baum im ohr!*"
—Rilke, *Die Sonette an Orpheus*

I stand inside the white pine, braced against the trunk,
head a bird, hands needles, sometimes an hour or what
you call time when you can't count, ignored by what
or whatever, a planting, a co-tree, its consciousness

in human form, an inflected self hoping to become
what it is or feels itself to be but not to think of what it is,
just the last chance to turn away, back to where we once were,
fragrant, green, head a longing realized somewhere else,

all sense, a love focused, not to be a tree but not oneself,
no antecedent, no purpose, but desire that lay in wait until
it grew a tree to be in, looking out as a branch to touch air,
the world mediated as wind, leaving you as you were

but not the same, here where you can't lie down so
look up through the branches, here where you stand
in perspective, the height you need to know, so you
stand still and listen to the silence in silence and this

you've come to hear, the hollow rich reverberations
all around where nothing happens, where the world opens
out to itself so you can go on forever, where there's
a tree surrounded by other trees but this is the tree

you want, the one you stand in as in a flame, and you
flare within it, no one would know the difference,
if they saw anything at all they would just see a tree,
they wouldn't see you, they wouldn't even look twice.

PROOF

After rain I walk down the path, looking about, roots
and rocks, birds, staring into the trees, probing. But
"looking", Plato's highest sense, still doesn't give me

proof and I feel a bit like his Lydian shepherd who
could see everything at a distance and was touched by
nothing, so decide again to give a chance to Aristotle who

said, "touch knows difference," and am about to go touch
trees, trace leaves, stick fingers into bark I might even
lick and bite, the way a dog or baby takes in the world,

when I think that perhaps Plato was right, touch is of
the senses lowest, a "mediating membrane," but then
remember how the Buddha, challenged by Mara to reveal

his authority, simply bent over and touched the ground,
which I'm about to do when the scent of damp earth
floods my senses, and there's nothing to prove.

SUNDAY OUT OF NOWHERE

The clock on the church tower is so simple
its difficulties come from elsewhere, from
curving the dial inward with a broken arm
to bumpy bits in air, even loose bells. No matter
how well-meaning God may be he is still God
and destined to the absolute which means we are
pretty much left on our own so the ordinary even
unpleasant past from a distance looks loved
only because it is complete and if it was going
to hurt us it already has and we are still here.
The clock pulses as if it were a facet of language,
syllable by syllable, building, so when we say
"it pulses," that's what it does, though it does
another thing which could be expressed another
way or not at all, as if we wanted it to mean more,
the way when something pressed to the wall pushes
back, broadening the base of its being, and ours
as we respond, respecting it, figuring out like me
what's what and what isn't, for the seasons change
fast as I look out over a playground now an ice-rink,
over lopped London plane trees to the power-station
that exploded in the last storm surge when seawater
reached a giant boiler and I thought we would all die
as it all ticks down pretending to be just the clicks
and chirps of sparrows, a drip drip, and all Sunday,
out of nowhere I found myself weeping so I couldn't
turn back, waiting for something while strangling
myself with the phone cord trying to get on as if there's
anything to get on with, like one of those trees, just
doing it, the clock banging on, or be a place where
you can be your own guest so there's no need to be
polite and you can tell the truth and even say Fuck Off
without giving offense, you who are fucking off.

THE CRASH

I went into the ditch after turning over and over
before settling, bursting into flames and watched

from far through the smoke, beautiful, the infinite
purposelessness of beauty, consuming time, exploding

tires as August whipped stones so they too caught fire
and I flew over it all, husk discarded, like smoke away,

out of sight, out of it, to drift down, glowing from the cold,
empty, to where I'll have to live on what I am now.

NIGHT

"…to find a form that accommodates the mess…"
—Beckett

Windows fallen away, you can't tell
where you or anything ends or begins, edges
folded in, no middle, so to hold you spread
into yourself where what's to go on, the
room gone, a flat shot of itself, dimensionless,
no portents, no gifts, you're stuck with each
piece not even itself, not even the space
between, there is none and you still reach
out with this weight in your chest, incubus
racking your ribs as it would take you
off but you cannot be found, not
even an outline, shadows of a shadow,
but—there, what's left as you move
your hand to trace dark's edges, not
entirely human, entirely human, what
by day you can forget, but not night.

ARS MORIENDI

LEGERDEMAIN

To shine, invisible, the door open
and no one there, to lie a shadow

on the grass, the abstraction of the visible,
watching and not seen, without conviction,

without opinion, disappearing like holding
the breath forever, always the same thing,

no name, the dark object light waves bend
around, to be the light paralyzing attention

so it arrives at the eye without exciting
the regard of the soul.

ACROSS GALAXIES

> *"Spooky actions at a distance"*
> (Einstein)

I could almost hear it when I listened
and still didn't take it for granted so that's

how it became luminous, coming at me
from way back as if it was lights down

a long alley or an afterimage of the unseen,
a crescendo of distance ticking like clockwork

over blue snow-fields rocking themselves shut
and *Not yet, not quite yet* I would say, parting

syllables as if swimming through to get
to the other side under safer skies always,

despite everything, stone-cold sober to
engineer my way to where opposites lean

in to keep each other up while behind them
float particles that have interacted in the past

then moved apart, but if you can still touch one
its partner dances instantaneously no matter

how far away, even at the other side
of the universe, even across galaxies.

THE SELF

can not be seen but is in everything so it all probably needs captions or an instruction manual as if there were still frontiers to cross but thieves had made off with baggage, documents and name-tags.

*

Among the self's provisions are brilliances that look like fruit, globes of fleshly flashes, blooms that poke through the weave, so eloquent it wants to eat them, so quiet but it thinks they're there and it can find them.

*

The self assumes dead birds scattered along the sand must have assumed something that was wrong. But for now, from a distance they seem a florescence, a growth, as if something had been accomplished the self can use.

*

The self makes a sketch of flowering shrubs, corridors through dogwood leading to a rickety barbed-wire paling on top of a stone wall, nailed to maple posts gone gray and spindly, something to love, needing repair.

*

So it switches on its flashlight and picks out everywhere like flames, bites in the dark, and keeps on going until the dog runs back and drops something at its feet.

*

For the self, any piece of a hologram will grow an entire image for it knows things want it as much as it wants them.

*

The bird's notes climb then swoop, then climb again, a glissando taking the self with them, lifting it so looking back it can glimpse that though the world is spirit it leaves a track and the track's it.

(ii)

POND

I watch as he floats up from the deep dark center, his gold
growing slowly more intense, glowing through the surface

where mayflies rise and fall. There seems nothing for him
to live on, just mud that absorbs everything, reflects nothing,

and here he'll stay in this pond deep in the woods, circling
where someone dumped him before dropping down to

the bottom, outlast winters that lock up. When snow turns
everything to snow you'll know he's there, iced in, waiting.

THE ANT

I sat watching him play a crazy tic-tac-toe
on the bathroom's floor tiles, zigging,
zagging, tracking, back-tracking,
doodling, speeding up, slowing down,
breaking all the rules so he can never win
except perhaps in his own mind, dashing
along a grout-alley, aha, direction, but
no, he's off again on some detour in
a tour where all is detour, *if he comes*
any closer I'll show him checkmate"
I say because he's making me nervous
and distracting me from the business
at hand, then suddenly he does a 180
and heads off as if he's found something
he didn't even know he was looking for,
his own trail, perhaps, a scent laid down
half a second before, a Eureka moment,
but no again, false alarm, false trail, he's
back, now if only he'd sit still a minute,
wait for things to sort themselves out, think
things through a bit, but no, he's off
dashing here and there as if there is a trail
neither of us knows that's worth looking for
and there's only so much time to find it, so
when he gets close I tear off a sheet, bend
down and hope I got him. I drop him
in it. OK, I say, as the heavens open,
fear death by drowning. He swirls, and
is gone. But how is it that, when I look
at the floor, there he is again, or someone
very like him, making a dash for wherever
he doesn't even have in mind?

THE GUMSHOE

Around my mountain garden dug from hard-pan scratch,
what's left of dryads still hang out, eating brightness out of air,
while in dust and rock weeds feed their fires, calling *more,*
more, more, as they shoulder their way through fence and gate
to take their place and keep me on my toes ready to wrestle
angels burly as rutabagas, tall as tomatoes, track down slug
and snail, outwit groundhog, vole and deer, until when pumpkins
glow across autumn nights and scarlet runners hang from
strings like Chinese lanterns, I lean against my rake and
light up like a gumshoe in a novel who found out no one
done it and put the case to bed, and I listen to the young
seeds' thin sopranos, creak of tree-roots gripping down
again for the long haul, hear the laughter of plump worms.

WALL

A chipmunk dives into the old stone wall
I'm on, his home and harbor, taking

what's given, navigating crevices smooth
as air. I love him, the wall's lymph, its

voice—listen! flowing through everything,
calling you to find the ventriloquist so

you follow what you can't, through halls,
down corridors, by hanging gardens, onto

vistas he gives you opening onto new angles.
If souls exist, he's one.

TO A MOCKINGBIRD

eager as a squirrel in leaflitter,
scratching up a brushpile, flash

of white, snagging worm, beetle,
beakful of moss for the nest,

running and hopping so fast
among rocks he's floating, and

now he's on a low branch with
cat, cricket, ungreased barrow

wheels, gun-shots, lawn mower,
tanager, and you listen, trying

to sort what's what while he sits
there pouring out whatever

comes to mind, until, a breather,
but there he goes again, jumping

off a quarter note into a world
where even as you watch and

listen you can't tell what is
and what's his.

THE SWAN

Through the open window comes "America" again, played in the park
by a Marine band among statues, one a large bird trying to leave

the stone, and then there are the voices of the couple upstairs who
have installed a new oven, it's all they talk about, new oven, how

it will change their lives. Meanwhile, my wife who is cooking
a late-life baby reports that the foetus is musical and kicks, so while

I walk on eggshells and wait, our blastospheric dot, our tiny gemule,
perfect little ballerina, is knotting herself into herself, rhyming with herself,

singing to the sonogram, dividing and dividing week by week, month
by month, and as I look out the window at the bird in the stone, I recall

Pavlova's last words, *Hand me my swan costume*, and await her debut
with a new song on new wings.

DEER WOMAN

What did she see to turn away
so sharp into deeper woods

after coming so close, standing
one foot raised, legs trembling

like light? Staring, what did she
make me—a sensation in

the silence, an agitation in air,
breathing bush, misplaced tree?

I could see inside eyes that cast
me back even when she turned,

ran off, stopped, looked round,
lingering sideways in sun-slant,

lonely as the deer-woman in
the story who married the hunter.

IN PLACE

I watch her leave down the drive, hang left, gone,
pick her out where the road rises and she moves
against snow coating the mountainside, past bare
apple-trees she emptied some weeks back, climbing
slowly upward, becoming cedar she's lost in, emerging
briefly by the stone wall that drives straight up, where
we saw the bear, walking over the roof of the ruined barn,
along past the white house that almost isn't there, and its
large dogs that are, then the slow climb south until she's
lost in broken landscape and I have to follow blind to
where I think she will emerge and turn downhill, past
a farm for sale, before backing round north, along the
Red Kill and another dairy farm for sale, to reappear later
through our woods, growing from speck to spinnaker
as she billows back up the drive, gathering everything
into her again so when I turn my eyes to where she's been,
yes, it's all still there, in place, but now it's also somewhere
else, as, known again, in her it settles back, gathered up,
and I can settle too.

TAKING THE SUN IN A CARPARK BESIDE THE EAST RIVER

My wife and I lie beside the five old regulars whose zinc lips
are white as Jolson's. Coconut drifts from their naugahyde skins

while her gold lamé hip pushes out Brooklyn, blocks Queens. To wafts
of talcum powder, seaplanes slalom over the thighs of this nymph

from a Pompeiian garden and splash down behind her face reflected
in a pool of last night's rain. Giant chimneys of Con Ed's 14th Street

power station cough and huff as the five old men become five
old cars that become five old sunning ladies parked in one spot,

while behind us on the FDR Drive up against the sky traffic whirls
round and round the island. I drop my eyes to the grit and glass

that glint like heaven's floor. When I raise them I see a cormorant
from another age diving for sustenance in water close to black.

SHE LIES BESIDE ME

To my daughter on the sea-floor, to the way
she married someone unknown to me
and left which was when I let myself know
I was in love with her in an old-fashioned way
just as she was beautiful in an old-fashioned way,
full figure and green like the plaster statue of
the naked reclining woman on the sideboard
when I was a kid, beside the fishbowl with
the goldfish, round and round till I got dizzy,
watched through the bowl to be her, mermaid
quivering in the currents, blinded by the light
through stained glass, yes, my daughter I took
for granted, to the way I saw rare migrating birds
the morning after they crashed into my windows
at night, to the way she told me she was getting
married in Sweden and then I was angry, jealous
as a cat, for he didn't deserve her, whoever he was,
she could do and knew so much, more than I,
and it was now all for someone else so I'd have
to tell her I was in love with her to keep her
for ever but instead I told her smoking was bad
and she had to stop though I knew she wouldn't,
and her marrying someone her own age was a slap
in the face, I might as well be dead as again I watch
her swim naked in the bowl, glorious though inclined
to weight which I hope swimming will keep off
at least for a while until she returns because now
I'm afraid that if I turn around she won't be there,
and why in Sweden? I think, maybe because she
looks like Ingrid Bergman or Anita Ekberg and
I can see her in something like "Smiles of a
Summer Night," though she should watch out
for those meatballs, and why did she leave without
even a note, I didn't know she'd gone but soon

found out and followed to a center for spiritual
growth that included sauna and Nordic track and
yoga to discourage ego where things were so arranged
that I was only allowed to watch by looking into
a floor-to-ceiling mirror behind the wooden benches,
sitting with my back to her to discourage intimacy,
watching reflections, which was getting nowhere so I
decided to return home but found I had no money,
just a credit card, and the barman gave me a strange look
as if he thought I'd paid but wasn't sure, and I too wasn't
sure but pretended I had, and kept drinking, to them all,
Mona and Myra, gorgeous blonde Finns, all of twenty,
you couldn't tell them apart, who took me everywhere
with them, at thirteen surviving my first nocturnal
emissions, awash in love and confusion, confused
with worship and erections, and to Agneta who I
imprinted on a bit later, hair long and thick as
a mermaid's, wondrous breasts she went home with
to Gothenberg one Christmas but returned without,
which I didn't understand but thought had something
to do with over-exercise, and who brought me back
a SKF ball-bearing key-ring I still have and spin.
They have never changed. I will always be walking
with them. Where did they go not to grow old?
And now she has come home, my daughter, back to me.
I watch as she sleeps in bed beside me, gold hair
in ripples over the pillow, shining even before dawn,
breath regular, luxurious, Aphrodite of the foamy sheets,
I peeping Pentheus. When she wakes, she will go to
the kitchen, make breakfast, the same each day, for ever.
Today, I will take her to look at the basil just germinated
on the windowsill. I don't ask her what she's thinking
because it is what I think, I know where she will go
and what she will do when she leaves because she is
still with me, and I don't ask where she's been
because I was there too, as I raise my glass to
my daughter, all hers, all her, all of her.

THE SNAKE

             long as my bootlace, thumb-thick, whips in front across
my path, a flick like memory, a curl, lightning so fast it

isn't there, green as the beans in cans just salvaged from my
mother-in-law's Brighton Beach apartment which we had to

clean out, cupboards, drawers stuffed with empty glass jars,
plastic containers and bags, bananas set to ripen under armchairs,

cans of carrots, peas, cut beans from Meals-on-Wheels—There!
A shiver I probe into, through dead leaves under bushes, into

duff and dead twigs, into old snake-hoarded earth, trying to peel
it back, and finding my mother picking at her thumbs so they bleed,

bobbing in her rocking-chair made from a pre-war leather car-seat,
and I'm stuck on my knees in musty humus thinking *I'm hungry*,

looking harder for what I'm not sure but know I won't find
though it's always there.

SALT

From the window I can see the TV someone dumped
off the bridge, cathode shattered, screen, among rocks.

On the table behind me, winter tulips shipped special
to bloom at Christmas, each trained up the spout

of its own plastic tube. I am wearing my long-dead
father's suede-fronted smoking jacket, stroking it first

down, then up, with, against the grain, each motion
erasing the other, like things leaving us we never had,

like a child going to a flower and returning less intact,
the scent tainting his life the way something sweet is soon

rotten, the way this street is white as the salt of Carthage.

HIGH COYOTES

A loud plane crumples air over our house which only sees
a low-flying chopper from time to time scoping things out.
We haven't even thought of planes since they said one crashed
somewhere in these mountains and all sorts of police, local,
state, reservoir and even the sheriff, sober for a change, a fire truck
and an ambulance rolled up our driveway asking if we'd found
anything recently on our land. "Anything?" "Bodies. Wreckage.
Anything." "Well, just a few deer bones," I said, "some gnawed
down to slivers. Some bear prints and coyote poop full of seeds
and hair and, oh, an anthill savaged by said bear." As they left,
"Hide the pot," I stage-whispered to my wife, and when they turned,
"Just kiddin'," I said, then "Look out for the high coyotes."

NEIGHBORLY

Since she bought the place a month ago, I've watched her
on her mini-tractor cutting till noon, when she switches and
weed-whacks till dark, the whacker strap across her body, a bandolier,
one of Goya's soldiers or Brady's drummer-boys. She takes
everything down, scythes in sweeps, and when she has the time
scours the streambed "to keep the pond clear," she said at our
one meeting when she said she was "an artist" from the city,
her English friend too, whom I've yet to see maybe because
she requires "frequent naps." So it's all on her to keep the place
in order, including the two yappy Chihuahuas, "rescue dogs."
The blackberry bushes are gone, brier patches, blueberries
and huckleberries I picked. She didn't know what they were,
she said. She thought it was all "weeds," ferns and goldenrod,
clover, timothy, elder, mullein, pokeweed, the whole shebang.
She has done a lot to see all around and through the few trees
that remain on her "park-like acres," even knocking down
an old stone wall. Now nothing can come at her without
her seeing, though with those headphones on she's deaf.
And there's still no end in sight, for by the time she gets to
the far end of her property down the hill, and climbs back up
the "weeds" have started to grow and need attention. And
I do too, standing there out of breath, "an old stone-savage
armed", and out of breath, but yelling. She unplugs, says
she's very sorry at what the dogs have done, and will put up
a good fence, "an invisible electric fence." Would I like some tea?
I drop the bamboo pole behind my back. I'd come prepared
for war but "O, well," I say, "it's just a garden." Then, "what
kind of tea?" neighborly, hoping the coyotes get them both.

THE GAZE

I say I love birds but down by the pond they fly in yelling as if it was war
or a public execution complete with beheading, drawing and quartering,
the whole shebang, until I can't take it any more. So I throw down my pen
and dash out in my pyjamas, shouting and waving my arms,
wishing I held with guns. They ignore me as if I wasn't there.
More pile in as a car drives down our red-dirt road. The driver waves.
I point to the trees. She points to my pyjamas. She is laughing.
I pick up stones but can't reach the birds who ignore me so I give up
and sit on a rock baked in the mid-day sun as they ride pine branches
like tornadoes, screaming for blood like sociopaths. Then—a great wind
as they rise as one and head off in their movie Indian calls to raid
another homestead, and I sit in their silence, feeling a bit foolish,
stones at hand, looking up over the pond at unburdened trees
then down at me and my pjs in the pond, and thinking,
What would Lawrence have done if, instead of a snake
"like a king" he was faced with a rude ruck of common crows?
How would he have found his way out of this "barbed-wire enclosure of
Know Thyself"? And how can I possibly feel myself "honored"
to know these crows? Suddenly I'm aware of being watched,
something is watching me. I look up and there on a branch
not a body-length away, he has me in his eyes, fixed in a gaze
distant as a star, and I can't move. I wait for what he has in mind.

AUBADE FOR AUTUMN

Light comes put-putting in
like—*No. Start again.* This

morning arrives almost before
light itself. *Not bad. Again.* This

morning is a sonata. *Better.* Telemann.
In G minor. *Good.* Organ adagios

of bronze and red cascading from
oak and maple. Trumpet the quick

fingers of aspen, and the slant eastern
light swarming down the dry stream-bed

like trail-bikes, two or even three up,
buzzsaws gone loco— *Calm down.*

Again. Trumpet is light embedding
itself inside the still green foliage of

young elms, whose leaves make lenses.
The silver echoes are drowned out by

damn dapple-dawn-drawn Honda ATVs—
Oh, pride, plume, here buckle! AND— .

*Slow down. O,—Pp! Legato! Start
again! Da capo!*—hell!

THE REDCOAT'S REVENGE

Evening is amplified drums and guitars, a thump
thump thump of electric bass, until at night just
as I'm falling asleep, they set off fireworks and soon
I'm choking on burnt tires, charred flesh, sulfur.
I get up, stumble over and bang on their gate:
Stop the damn noise! No one answers but I think
I hear someone say "the Limey" before the noise
gets louder, then more Roman candle flares, bombs
bursting in air, rockets' red glares, a ratchet of Chinese
firecrackers and then explosions with enough force
to bring down mountains. I slink back. It seems hours,
but eventually, head under pillow, I do fall off
the edge into sleep. But then I'm woken by the silence.
They must be sodden on the kitchen floor or passed out
over their barbecue or fallen into the goldfish pond
they stock and the mink empties. I get up again and
go out on the deck into the dark where stars pop overhead
and a satellite or two skim close as fireflies. This black
silence is a bit unnerving, so I sit in the railings to think
of setting their place on fire and blaming a stray rocket.
I get so caught up with the idea I almost fall back and
over into the bushes where it might take weeks or even
months for the cops to find the body, and when they do
they'll blame the neighbors and haul them off and
that will be that, normal again.

COMPANIONS

"Clear off my land!" I yell. They look around, then
stomp off over the rise where they whang a jay
to pieces. Everything is theirs. They have inherited

the earth, even the insides of my house which they
once strewed under pines and tossed into the old quarry
among tiles, broken glass, tires and iron bedsteads.

This land's been cleared more than once. Clear-cut and
blasting powder took off tops, wedges along bluestone lifts
turned pre-Devonian seas to right angles for city streets.

But at night sometimes there's fur along the cabin's sides,
great galaxies howling overhead, stars diving over earth
like birds and in the morning I can feel my skin close

round boulders smooth as apples, watch shadows and
images stretch across snow-fields, companions, analogies.

HERE'S

       home for burnt poppies spread out, a frisson, a
goddess' skirts. In the old apple-tree birds clatter like boards

until, silence: Look. The moon is rising, a flower in a ghost's hand,
Yupik mask carved into its own dream, floating in night sky

where once among fireflies, shivering moon, stars, northern lights,
scented ecstatic spirits unmoored in all directions, I swam.

COYOTE

He traps and eats a butterfly, snaps at his mate who
nips his heel and off they go on a chase just as the wind
gets up the ponderosa, few clouds over the plateau
laid out green below and the Sangre de Cristo range opposite
played over by brilliance that comes and enters the stones
at my feet, shining out through them so they are light,
and the world is lovely until all at once everything goes out,
cancels, falls apart in some dark cloud from nowhere,
so while everything before had seemed possible now
nothing does and you don't know where you are, or who,
or why, and then you remember Coyote who carved
figures from wood, tossed them in all directions saying:
Come to life. Do what you want, then took off laughing
all the way to Hiroshima where in one instant
the flash cast people's shadows in concrete
and turned their bodies to vapor.

YOU COULD DRIVE ALL THE WAY TO ALASKA

and not know it, she said. The road draws you on.
Any place to stop has been and gone before you can
make up your mind. It's like "The Red Shoes".
Put on a car and you can't stop moving. *Minnows—*
100 Feet. Night Crawlers. Worms. Shiners. Suckers.
In a split second women in curlers, scarves across
the curlers, dance across the screen. You're driving
too fast, she says. In creative driving, she continues,
you bring the land up ahead of you gradually,
like film titles. You are not driving creatively.
Hunting preserves blur behind barbed wire.
In the middle of nowhere airplanes land on a lake.
Motor boats drag skiers. Nowhere is inaccessible.
High on the shining wall of a savings bank
the true time and temperature in F and C.
Billboards abuse the devices of poetry until a spa
slows things down to a strong saline spring
sputtering laboriously from a corroded tap a man
brings his evening cup to, fills it, sits down on
a bed of flowers, lights a cigarette, drinks to
his health. We almost go crashing through evening
and out the other side, but instead spin into a motel
driveway through bright OPEN signs but on the
office door it says *closed.* The car in exhaustion
comes to the end of its reel. What's left coils
on the floor as two old ladies stagger out and
invite us in. They sip whiskey under a tiger head.
Next morning we're off again where crows big
as roosters confederate on verges or stand over
scraps on the blacktop. The way is marked by
the reluctant ascension of crows, progress timed
by small squashed mammals at the side of the road.
The miles tick by till noon. The highway speeds up
and vanishes over the next hill. You vanish too
into a distance you have no time to remember.

EXPLORERS

Talliers of date and hours, determiners
of altitude by Polaris or Aquilae, longitude

and latitude by immersion and emersion
of the sun's lower limb or the dark limb of

Jupiter's first satellite, they measured, they coped,
boiling and stretching powder horns, scraping

and stretching them on wood, heating buffalo glue
by *bois de vache* to repair barometers and whatever

broke, over killing snows laid down glassy grids
to make the air fit, edge to frozen edge.

THE BREAKS

Where willow, rose and snowberry grew, behind the
Rusted run of three-strand wire strung on bent steel poles
He dips water from the trough, tosses it in bright arcs
Onto his head. Down by the gulch, someone is singing
The same song over and over. Nothing moves in this
Cow-burned land. He leans against a broken binder
About to topple down a trampled bank. Crickets
In dry patches of bunchgrass fake and fade. Then there's
Just one. He listens, shakes his wet hair and heads on in,
Reminded of his mother's old black dog shaking off water
From the pond that July 4 while the band still played
As fireworks fizzled in the unexpected storm that made
The front of the house fly up like a tent flap, and above it all
One cricket called, a crisp run of syllables between flashes,
Its persistent trills speaking the stony land and a couple
Of flinty stars that as they rose clipped the mountains
From which thunder rolled with the weight of old machines,
And the radio crackled on until drowned out, signing off.

Part Two

SKY BURIAL

(Basil Bunting, 1900-1985)

At my beat-up maple writing desk, stuck,
I look out to maples turning red and find myself
remembering sitting with him among roses,
celandines, black and white crystals from a local
coal tip, looking down from Wylam, "place
of the water-wheel", to the once salmon-crowded
now frothy Tyne, "washing machines," he says,
sipping my gift of Red Label from a mug taken
from a bar with no bottles. "Principle?" "Penury."
He moves, groans. "You know, in the Sudan
they put men down at seventy and eat their women
as soon as they become grandmothers. In Tibet
when you die they chop you up and leave you on
a mountain top for vultures, 'sky burial', so you
end up as vulture dung, your epitaph." As we watched
a train worming its way from one side of England
to the other, a seagull flew over and shat on his shoulder.
"That's good luck," he said, wiping it off with a tuft
of grass and tossing it down the hill. "I've had a
twenty-line poem on my desk five years now waiting
for the last line—and I just found it."

THIS HOUSE

When I get to the dining room and its three fish
trapped in a bowl I take off my boots and go barefoot
into the parlor with its birds in cages singing so loud
I can't hear myself think, so I go to the library where
I can be with Scott of the Antarctic and his son Peter
who, before the war, gave my aunt a signed watercolor
of ducks, some geese, in flight. I'd nailed it to the wall
next to a print of Brice Marden's "The Muses," a frieze
of green, white, green, blue loops evoking a procession
of Zeus' daughters who we follow one way and then
reverse the flow and start again at the other end.
I'm thinking that Memory is the mother of the muses
when a stone crashes through the glass and lands
under the desk. I look through the broken pane at a boy
running off. A bell rings but nothing happens. I light
a cigarette though I don't smoke. I'll change my shirt,
I'll change my shorts. What holds them up? Memory?
I'll change my life. I'll write it down. I look for a note-pad.

NOTE 1: Day-Trip

A small steam engine is pulsing at rest in the middle
of the viaduct over the Derwent at Rowland's Gill.
Women are taking off my clothes for a shivering
cousin Neil who has just charged down the bank
and fallen into the river, practicing to be a drunk
on an oil platform in the North Sea where clothes
would be useless when they fished him out and
laid him on the rig where he is now just a memory
of a summer day where one boy falls and another remembers.

LOOKING FOR THE LOST

How what you are stands less clear than the fresh-turned earth
  because there's a death inside us that's more than crooked
sleep though we still want to love the body— how I used
  to love my body, which is to say the sunlight and low angles
of dark and how I fear it now, the way it changes so that hand
  reaching out before my eye is stained and spotted like time itself,
like the memory of time, marsh miasma, someone else's
  simultaneous mummy. I don't understand, so how can I trust it?
And yet this hand and its companion, while not perfect make do
  as a serviceable hybrid that chugs along and bottoms out
from time to time but that's part of it, the life you've known
  though you can't really root for it any more, it has its limits,
it's only there a certain way, if done right, for a short time, so
  when you get a certain age and look back it all looks accident
and yet at the same time inevitable, so you keep working at what
  you don't quite have hoping, when the time comes, it will still
work for you. There's a lot more to it for there are always questions,
  always more hands to reach out and back through the open windows
where the passenger train is itself the scenery we watch from,
  black fields moving on what were rich fens, deep, but now
drained to the price paid of silver coin for haring-silver, segge-silver,
  dust rising east in a wind from the Urals blotting out the track,
the land shrinking and dropping, though still how beautiful,
  shining loam, bright sillions, even if no more islands to reach up
and hold onto so you're left holding your own shoulders in your
  old hands, muscles taut, the land posed like von Hagens'
"Yoga Baby," skin framed in situ, identity "not provided", alive
dead, dead alive, vivid docetic, plastinates adding "Pregnant Woman
  with Foetus," carved with the maker's signature, and a room at
the end, "Visitors May Choose Whether Or Not to Enter This Room,"
  where we find "The Wonders of Human Development," flute music
piped in. What development? Who should see this? "Anyone interested
  in learning what makes us human." Is it art? Is it science? Is it
a funeral parlor, moving objects constantly multiplying themselves,

mirrored taxidermy, moving away from oneself into oneself,
so where have we gone? Let us look. There are always questions,
    everything incongruous, as if our ambition is to be invisible,
anywhere and everything, alter egos with alter egos, posed and
    invested in attributes, time as anacoluthic, everything at once,
trying to beat it with whatever comes to hand, not philosophy's
    isolation of the concept but a dream of particulars, not so much
ague and hacking cough as pike jack-knife, even a diorama flash
    of teal, neck-dips, distant down-notes, splash and drift of tench,
corncrake's *crax, crax,*, bittern's bassoon in reeds, "bumping", the
    speaking marsh new-coined from sounds themselves cast from
air's core, where lilies' lamps shake so shine rings out at wind's
    swipes of alder scattering flower heads, numb in the spinnies,
buckthorn, marsh thistle, crusts of blue flag and a gust tracing across
    itself, across the mere, whiff of cow-tad, turve-fires, fish blood in
barrels, path through the carr petered out in oatgrass until the moon
    opens quicksilver, guilder-rose, a splash where night's full
of rotten harrs, boggles and wandering lights, reason enough for
    some to have drained this place, and as it turns in cuts, sluices,
clows and sasses I marvel here in the Catskills with a boy's wonder
    at the Claud's great driving wheels hauling "The Fenman"
over black fields toward Lynn and look out the window at all this
    and the old fen slodger with terrible catarrh who wandered into
the ER saying his foot "itched" after he stuck a spike through it
    years ago, but when we peeled off the filthy bandages the itch
was maggots, the itch gangrene. Everything had passed him by and
    not much meant. All my life I have looked for the lost, and lost.

WAVES

On the sea-shore I watch three children
running and playing against the wind as

white birds hover and dive. Three women
run behind the children, laughing, skirts hoisted,

tucked into their knickers. Over the waves
I hear their rolled "r's", the sound I love,

what Defoe called our "shibboleth," and
the smallest woman picks up a large stone,

weighs it, then flings it far as she can where
the ocean closes over, and it's gone.

NO CIGARS

—for Jack Wesley and Hannah Green

"Great clouds," I say, looking out across the studio
when a breeze blows its yellow scent of broom up
from Cagnes onto a corner of the canvas where sky
will be. "Looks OK," says Jack. "Did I tell you
I worked for Boeing? There," he dabs. "You have
to find a way to keep sky up. Clouds do that."
Silence. Jack is mixing paint. I sit remembering
when I brought my father my first book, inscribed
to him, neatly wrapped. He opened it, stared.
"What's this?" he said. "A *book*?" It flew across
the room. "I thought it was a box of cigars."
"Boeing?" I said. "Yes. Flying machines." "My dad
was an engineer. He admired accuracy and precision.
He also loved art. He even copied Manet's 'Déjeuner,'
made the frame and hung it on the wall. When I
found you in one of his art books and told him
you were my friend, that was the only time I ever
impressed him with anything. He even said he would
read my book." "Did he?" "He did not."

PLACES OF POWER

I received daily French lessons from one of his nurses
on a bench in the grounds of the Vence sanitarium
where he died, hero of my youth, author of the one novel
my father read ("sex sells—you should write like him"),
whose *Sons and Lovers* I made my mother read, and whose
trajectory I followed, seeking the same sun in Italy, France,
Mexico old and new, finally to Taos where in 1930
his ashes were left on the station platform by quarreling
Frieda and Mabel, where years later I picked them up
and took them to the ranch to scatter again under the large
pine behung with "various odds and ends of iron things"
that shaded the enclosure where a coyote pair dashed about
and where stinging dust blew into my face so everything
began to look different, running into each other, and the top
of that ocote pine floated like a blue cloud of female rain from
blue San Felipe sky, or water climbing back up, shivering
like the paper-bark banners Chichimecas stuck into the ground
or wedged between rocks to signal places of power.

MY FRIEND, THE OLD SAILOR,

had a green parrot on his shoulder
that could have been a second head

speaking Guaraní. At night
he took off one skin to reveal

another. His wife had no English,
braided thick black hair down

to her waist, each night plunging
her hands into his deep plumage

while the parrot flew overhead
singing love-songs in four languages.

Then one day they said a sudden
wind had swept him up from inside

so he raged into the hallway, setting
about doors and windows with a

fire-extinguisher, cursing those who'd
carried yaws and VD to paradise,

until they caught and carried him to
his room from which that night he

flew with the gorgeous parrot on
green wings. His wife soon followed.

LIMONI

In this fjord town, bells from the wooden church
strike sometimes before, sometimes after,
sometimes even on the hour.
                    A few days ago
I found a beat-up alarm clock on the street and stuck it
in my sock drawer where it erupts at random.
                               Now I watch
drops gather along the lintel, plump up, fall and shatter at
an even pace. Through the cold mist I can just make out
the statue that has never been identified satisfactorily,
feet and hands gone. Pigeons fly on and off, on and off.
I call him Olaf.
                    Sometimes, writing at my desk, the room
fills with a scent out of nowhere, rich as a Gobelin tapestry,
a Tallis motet. The place lightens like that time I stood
in Sicily, midwinter, alone above a nameless empty valley,
thinking summer, trees, and "limoni" I said. Slowly the word
suffused the air saffron as the sun that broke through, spilled
out, filling the valley, everything, with no time.

ESSAY IN TIME

I'm reading how Hawthorne saw maidens with pitchers
on their heads, midnight solitude with "untamable water

sporting itself in the moonlight," and I'm back decades
but with flashbulbs for moonlight and for maidens tourists

tossing coins into the Acqua Virgine Nicola Salvi used
for his firework machine that went up in flames to become

Trevi stone, Abundance and Health, "an essay in water,"
soon to be *acqua non potabile,* and still is, no doubt,

though now my slanty little goat eyes are peering again
through Etrurian shade to watch crystal contadine

bathe naked in a stream that falls in flames from them,
supple statues mocking time, and me.

WHAT GIVES

Old fruit in my garden bobs on the branch,
   human, stout. Crows fly in and
take it apart, the way ravens took apart
   dead warriors, going first for the eyes.
Over the hill, the tide goes in and out,
   a second theme related to the first.
Sun stuns the crows, it does not let them go.
   It does not let them through, they're *here*.
It is noon, Roman ghost-time though
   this is not Rome where I slept each day
till noon when the wind from Ostia
   came through the broken windows and
woke me up. I dreamed in Rome of Rome,
   where I don't know where I am.
Clothes on the roof across from me
   billow out and a lovely woman
rearranges them with one hand, the
   other holding down her orange skirt.
Later, she and I will meet and at Veii,
   by tombs, by ancient rock-cut sacred
bathing places, on the terra cotta earth
   that yielded statues of the Vulca School,
among nettles and daisies and buttercups,
   to the sounds of frogs and one cuckoo,
make love... Now there's a line of oranges
   left at the high-tide mark, blood oranges
from crates dumped or washed overboard
   in last night's storm . . .
                              One thinks of the human,
meaning the dailiness of things, a family's clothes
   on a line, oranges and crates of oranges,
tombs, frogs, cuckoos, the swelling sea,
   women, the wonder of women, the importance
of tomorrow which soon comes due, even here

71

in the mountains where each summer evening
I watch the waxwings find their way home
    heading west over my house, cheeping
as they fly, always a straggler or two trying
    to catch up and calling louder as the stars
begin to move in, or seem to, as they did
    at Veii, Cerveteri, Tarquinia whose augurs
turned them all, birds and stars, everything
    back or into the human, prognosticating the
true course and nature of things and on tombs
    had painted scenes more vivid than life itself
so what is left behind is not the world
    but some version of what it meant
to be alive, not what is given but what gives.

SANTA MARIA DELLA CONCEZIONE DEI CAPPUCCINI

Bones in bone coffins, hearts
   of ribs, rib clocks and
     armbones pointing to
the full hour, an hour-glass sternum,
   an entire skeleton
     in the ceiling holding a balance
of bone, a scythe of scapulas,
   a skull flying with scapula wings,
     a frieze of jawbones,
all round the lower world where
   I walk on dust carried
     from Palestine, here
where beauty is death's joke
   and the joke's on me.

OUR LADY OF THE CATS

"*Gatos en la columnas asombradas*,"
—Rafael Alberti, *Roma, peligro para caminantes*

I wait at the tail of a long line to pay my electric bill.
When I get to the window, it shuts. I join another line.

When I get to the window the teller is counting
a fat wad. "Buon——." She looks at the clock, slams

the window down. It all shuts down.
At the Largo Argentina, I lean over the railing around

the ruins of Four Republican Temples where an old lady,
skirts hoisted, hops nimbly slab to slab, calling for coins,

catching, chasing them under stones, then sits.
Calling in the cats to count and feed, she reaches under

a fallen column for a small jam jar, unscrews it, dips
a spoon in, probes under an ancient lintel for a new kitten

whose face she pushes gently into the spoon while it squirms,
then relaxes, sits back, slowly licking its lips. I drop a 500 lire

note that floats into her out-stretched hand, one note, then
another, and another. I will live in the dark a while longer.

THE MOON

Despite everything, it's still my birthday, so I whistle and sing silly
songs, old songs, *Here we go loopy-loo… O bella ciao, bella ciao,
bella ciao, ciao, ciao…* I'm happy in the kitchen, throwing together

my rat-tat-tat-touille made with whatever's ripe in the garden,
ennobling it all with handfuls of basil. Vasari lies on the couch,
under Gigli's *Diario Senese*. But books are graves. No books

for me, no recipes either. I'm making it all up as I go along.
They're not my books anyway. They're my wife's. She can read
later. Now it's party time. *Par-tay! Par-tay!* Just us two. *Here,*

*put on this funny hat. Try on this squash blossom. Here, hang these
scarlet fagioli from your ears. Look what a big zucchino I've got!*
At my age any pleasure's worth having. The body's still built for it,

the way the old chestnut trees were built for the full moon I watched last
night as they let go a bit at a time through gaps of broken branches
so she climbed up above the house, gathering herself to herself,

filling up as if to stay, moving into whatever space stars had left, so
they trailed after her like silver drones over vineyards where wild boars
rooted, over the partisan caves where porcupines gnawed chestnut

trees planted after the war, turning their spines into fireballs while
in the Radda churchyard she illumined the plaque to those
UCCISI DAI BARBARI TEDESCHI.

THE PALERMO ROAD

In memoriam Basil Bunting

Outside Trapani, snow on the mountains,
                    dark red earth,
            terraces, orange trees, cars following our
dust-cloud, we following theirs, others
                    overtaking and
            cutting in. A three-wheeler with a black pig
straining in a net, another with three
                    little girls giggling
            waving and choking on our dirt and fumes,
and Walter still fuming insisting on the daily
                    history lesson
            he's memorized: *Between the mouths*
of the Fiumara Zappulla and Capo D'Orlando
                    was in 1299
            fought a sea-battle in which... He slows
slower to think what comes next and a dignified
                    old man in a
            black suit with black armband overtakes us on
a donkey with wood planks strapped to its sides.
                    In Palermo
            a priest frowns when I ask, but points. We
find it after scrambling over iron railings
                    Judith gets
            hung up on and round walls W gets stuck
between: "Teatrino dei Pupi Armati,
                    Guiseppi Argento
            & Figli, Via del Pappagallo, 10."
We enter an empty barn with whitewashed beams,
                    a few decorations
            for Natale, '67, pictures of the palatins
in armor on the walls. A man motions us
                    to follow him

76

backstage and up a steep ladder past
grinning cannibals and Moors. At the top
                along the walls
                    puppets almost life-size, rods to hands
heads and legs, the oldest one, he says,
                one hundred years,
                    we can have for eighty thousand lire.
"Ecco Orlando!" A body with three heads,
                        boy, man,
                    old man, surrounded by shiny shields that
took a month to make. Back out front
                    the wooden benches
                    fill. Six people at five hundred lire each.
Against a painted backdrop and to music
                the story of Orlando
                    unfolds. You recognize him by his cross-eyed squint,
denoting ferocity. He comes to Charlemagne's court
                    to swipe some soup
                and vitals for his mother and sister hiding
in the rocks. He calls the emperor "Magnomagno",
                    "Eateat", and
                    runs away pursued by two retainers. When they catch
him he smacks them about until his ma
                recognizes them
                and they go back to beg pardon of the king
who knocks her down and Orlando knocks him down
                and yells:
                    "I'll kick him in the teeth and knock him out!"
Then Charlemagne forgives his sister,
                embracing her
                    too long for Orlando who yells, "Hey, *basta*!
Enough of that! Hey, break it up!" More battle scenes.
                Swords clash
            on swords and shields above the barrel-organ.
Saracens fall in heaps, and twitch,
                many with
                    their heads lopped off. One runs around

77

like a chicken with no head. And then
                    the action stops
           while the *puparo* runs from behind the scenes
to sort out boys scuffling with the organ-boy
                    for his job.
           The losers settle down to cigarettes and
hacking coughs. After, Walter's miffed.
                    "Why was there
           no Orlando going mad when Angelica
betrays him? I've read the book. He recovers
                    his lost wits
           by sniffing the urn they're in which Adolfo
brought back from the moon, and which…"
                    "Astolfo," Judith says,
           "not Adolfo." Next day we aim for Cefalù,
W mad because J still refuses to share a room,
                    and still upset
           because at a mosaic of a "*scena erotica*" in
Piazza Armerina of two lovers embracing,
                    she with her back
           towards us, drawing aside her gown to show
her arse, he said he saw J wink at me.
                    He drives his usual
           slow pace, and a donkey-cart with paintings
on its panels of knights and palatins, driven by a woman
                    who looks like
           Orlando's mother careens in front, finocchi bound
like fasces bounce and sway, radishes the size of beets
                    roll about
           as she swerves to avoid potholes and pits.
W curses in German and honks. "Cigarette!"
                    he calls to J who
           pushes in the dashboard lighter. When it pops out
she hands it to him. It's at his lips before
                    he screams
           and drops it in his lap, slamming on the brakes.

"*Mistück!*" J turns round to look at me,
                knowing my thoughts.
              A woman walks by in a large black straw hat,
from the top of which the white head of a cockerel
                protrudes and,
looking about, crows.

LA VIGLIA DI NATALE

Omeoteotl, the Aztec Lord of Duality, first
made the universe, then himself. Makes sense,
     I thought, walking at dusk in the lovely
Giardino Pubblico. What's the point of being
     if you have nowhere to be? Just then I smelled
honeysuckle where there was no honeysuckle,
     heard birdsong where there were no birds,
which a voice nearby found easy to explain:
     "All done by water-pipes."
                         The bonfire,
a huge tipi, sat ready in the piazza of this Sicilian town
     founded by the half-woman, half-bull atop a pillar
that looked taller than it was, "an old Greek perspective
     trick," said the voice, the crowd applauding
to the skirl of *cornamuse* when a priest lit the pile,
     heavy trunks leaning in all round, seeming solid but
which, the voice noted, wasn't, mostly small branches,
     twigs, refuse and straw which blazed up fast,
collapsing the logs inward, sending spark-showers
     everywhere like exploding stars, high as the
cathedral's square tower, over the pillar, then down
     onto and around our feet so we hopped about
trying to shake them off, stomp them out, flapping
     our arms to clear our clothes, swatting our heads,
slapping sides, until everyone was dancing a saltarello,
     leaping about, yelping as if we'd just invented
an ecstatic religion. "Not panic!" yelled the voice.
     "Sparks not burn!" before he too was flailing about,
almost knocking me over, he who had an answer
     for everything, making a dash for the church doors,
dropping his Baedeker.

RESTORATION OF A COPY OF AN IMAGINARY PAINTING

"*. . . dire, non pas tout crûment sa vision, mais par un transfert instantané,
constant, l'écho de sa présence.*"
—Victor Segelen

The white is meant to stabilize the house, but the matted crenellation
of reed-thatch throws it off to the side
until a squadron of crows solidifies the rhythm, carrying the eye through
incendiary doors to open space, opening it to the ancient, that is to say, the habitation
of sun and moon, the interior to the south, above the river that flows
by persimmon trees, over a statue with arms encircling a trunk, so you're not sure
who's upholding who, and the figure of someone silhouetted on a wall.
The month is September. Roses turn to the right,
and fail. Silent women in white blouses file by. But just at that moment when
the main matter seems to be about to be represented as rain and wings in a dark garden
and a bull bellowing, words like those that descended on the apostles are heard.
The copyist may have been about to make each tongue say the same thing,
but now it is too late. Everything before restoration is an unproven fact.
Everything after is guesswork.

AT SEGESTA

The temple, deserted, building unfinished,
mountains desolate and steep, blue flowers,
white stone, cow parsley, orange flowers
of the asphodel. I grip barbed wire, lean over,
watch crows circling, and below them
sheep like toys. Everything shines as
the blank rock outcrops turn back sun
so it's too much for the eyes. My ears fill
with silent spaces and my life comes up at me,
engulfing. *What are you doing here?*
I spin around. Just the wind in the weeds
and the temple behind pressing in on me,
so I go back, stand under the unroofed
space and unloosed wind. Stringy shadows
flow from the unfluted Doric columns as if
the wind, having blown down columns,
is trying now to blow their shadows down.

SEABIRD

Near Enna of Proserpina's rape and return,
on the beach at Isola Bella, collecting marble pebbles,

perfect artifacts of waves, a boy with hair blond
as wheat follows me, all gesture, urging quick

as a seabird something I don't understand, so I
brush him off, but later, turning, I see this boy in

the waves, looking back at me with the face I'll later
see in town, *Con gli angeli,* on a poster edged with black.

CYCLADIC MORNING, 1968

"With the gods overthrown like that, no one knew which way
to turn"
—Yannis Ritsos

Morning breaks, scattering light onto the mirror in which
a caique sails into view and a soft rain finds the scent of geraniums.

Silence is still on the marble stairs as the sun slowly shapes
the house on the cliff that was once a caldera's rim. This is

the house of the torturer who specialized in eyelids. He uses
katherevousa, strained of impurities, which no one understands.

I can just make him out, enemy of scuffs and scratches,
polishing his BMW so it gleams like his original Parthenon.

HYMN TO APHRODITE

"Anchises, why do you take me for one of the immortals?"

A caique sails into view on the mirror, and a light breeze
brings hyacinth and geranium through the open window.
Music like silence on marble steps. Doves.

Among flowers of the broom goats browse, bees hum.
In the garden, anemone petals are her fragrant clothing,
leaves her breasts, late violets are woven into her hair

so when she moves light as foam everyone wants her,
none more than I as we climb up into the olive grove
and sit on the side of an ancient trough carved with

the constellation Castor and Pollux, boxer and horse-breaker,
water splashing from a lion's mouth. She bends to take
from the basket a crisp blue cloth, spreads it, places

plums and greengages in the center, gives me a blue plum
I peel with my jack-knife, drop into a cup of retsina
to cool. In fall, her brothers string nets from tree to tree

for migrating quail, then pack them in cans of olive oil, seal
with a soldering iron. She unwraps one from grape leaves,
holds it to the sun, places part of a wing slowly on her tongue.

As day draws in, to be here is to be not here, to be bodiless is
to be here, here on the other side of shadow, the other side of here.

THE FOUNTAIN
Istanbul 1970

In memoriam Yaşar Kemal, 1922?-2015

"My mother was Circassian, born a slave, ashamed of my darkness.
'That's what happens when you marry a Turk'," she said. The door opens.

A man in a leather apron enters carrying a basket. "Today you are lucky.
Cherries have come, and peaches." The window opens to the south wind

backing up sludge. Beyond is the misty skyline of the Golden Horn.
She goes into the kitchen, comes back with a pie, "sour cherry."

"I will call Kemal for you." She dials, speaks, waits, puts the phone down.
"The exchange says he's changed his number. We all do. Have to."

She cuts the pie with a dagger. "He was sent to me. Lots of people are,
like you. He arrived at seven a.m., peasant time, 1951. His Kurdish

goat-felt jacket stank. That's the same stiff coat Paul begged Timothy
to bring him in jail. He stayed over a week. No concept of a visit."

An electric muezzin goes off. She pushes herself up from the chair.
"I'll try again." Same result. It's time to go. "Don't mention me by name,

and don't write about this visit. Next time I may not be so lucky.
If you want to meet again, it should be in Üsküdar, out in the open,

across from the ferry in Kabataş, by the fountain. I will try to bring him."
"Is it safe?" "He doesn't care. For a writer, he says, looking over your
shoulder is suicide. I will call you. Say "nevede çeşme? Where's the fountain?"

for Mina Urgan

THE VISIT

Communists are *"Commune-ists"*, Ankara still *"Angora."*
Her dearest wish is a Paddington apartment. As she talks
I look out from the rose-draped balcony under volutes, corbels,
lattices, through a huge pylon to tankers battling currents,
hammers and sickles on smokestacks. Trusting their own pilots,
they make a habit of ramming old wooden mansions, *yalis*.
Beside them wooden fishing boats bob like new moon arks.
"I put our own lemon juice in the jam to make it set. You can
still get strawberries from Arnavutköy." A newspaper lies open
at a street protest. "If students want guns I'd send them to the army.
They'd have guns then. When I first arrived Turkey was more romantic,
all fezzes and veils. Now I expect they'll soon burn down the yali
next door. The owner won't sell. They've burnt down all the others
and put up concrete terraced buildings. Excuse me." She waddles
to the phone, dials, slams it down, curses in Cockney Turkish.
"I've tried calling the grocer all day for strawberries. I'm ready
to throw the phone out the window. They brought a Froggie
in to mend the system. 'Ah, beautiful! Beautiful!' he said. 'Perfect.
Just leave it alone'. So now you can't use the damn things.
They're all dead. Everything's dead. Did Yildez tell you her
theater earnings have dropped to half under martial law? She's
too thin, married too young, works too hard. My other children—
my husband was a pasha—I met him when I was an actress.
His father was pro-British and sent him over to study electrical
engineering and marry an English girl. When Turkey went with
the Axis powers he had a heart attack and died. I was just a girl
when I arrived. They used to catch so many fish just over there
they had to throw them back. Do you like green fig conserve?
They still chuck back tomatoes. They don't know how to can them...
Ah, Turan!" She introduces me. He points to a stain on his new
white suit trousers. "Always look before sitting," he says,
sitting wearily. After a while he says, "Finally they're going
to produce my dramas on classical themes. Part one is 'Ibrahim
the Lunatic.' I'd been banned for criticizing Atatürk. But now

I've disguised him in my seventeenth-century trilogy, 'The Theme of Power'. If they see through it I'm done. I must make a phone call." As he rises into the light, scars shine on face and hands. I hear him dial, curse, slam the phone down. He returns with a bottle of Fruka. "Wrong number. A canteen and an earful of abusement. You can't trust the phone." They start to talk in Turkish. I look over the balcony. Seagulls. Cumuli accumulating. And below everybody doing something. I settle on a woman staggering under a bag of bloody bones, and a man crossing the street strapped to a huge pane of glass, looking as if at every step he is about to fall, but righting himself, stumbling, rights himself, staggers.

COLD POP

On the table I'm trying to balance a coin on edge.
Through the shack's one window the sea shivers.
In the sink a squid I bought but don't know what to do with

flops about. A pipeline brings water through the desert.
It arrives hot and gritty. I watch the salt-encrusted
rocks round which the tide drifts. It thunders. The locals

say spirits or seraphim or the like are passing by, which
is what I should have done. I imagine them with the wide eyes
of demented pigeons. By day I sit in sloppy surf and pay a boy

to bring me cold pop twice an hour. They say the natives
have no word for time, but down the road someone is
putting up a hotel bigger than this entire place. A few years

from now, it will be blown up with sacks of imported fertilizer.

TWO-HEADED DEER

"What we say on this earth is like a dream;
        We only mutter like someone waking from sleep.
Here none of us says anything real."
        —*Cantares Mexicanos*

For weeks I lived on gray-green buttons in deep caves,
in reflected sunlight that feinted across sun-soaked plazas

where air buckled, and below that I lived in vivid flowers
on vivid walls, white flowers carved to thick froth,

where I told a two-headed deer who was the woman
who left me that I loved her, tried to catch her as she leaped

like a shadow against the wall of the turquoise enclave
while quetzal plumes rained down, but "Not me," she said,

"these intoxicating flowers, not me, these songs in the house
of the green-swan cacao flowers or golden-flower bell-rattle

hummingbirds, the dancing transvestites with bird masks."
She laughed and vanished into the dark, into the eye's shadow,

the tear, the cricket repeating the same lonely phrase with
no reply over and over under my window.

IN THE SMOKING MIRROR

"the opaque obsidian mirror with its riddling dark reflections"
—Inga Clendinnen, *The Aztecs*

At the top of the ladder someone sits as if to get a better view.
"Are you looking at me? I say. "I wasn't," he says. I go
into the bedroom. She's asleep. I go to the medicine chest
and pour out a handful of painkillers. I return and jostle
her awake. "Every Thursday," I say "where do you go?
And why is he here?" "I live here too, you know,"
she mumbles. "You're never here." "Nor you."
Where does she go? Once I returned to find him under
my desk, rifling through my papers, looking for something.
What? More than once I've said "Get out and don't come back."
Next day I take the bus to El Pedregal, back to the rented
old house on frozen lava, chevron-shaped windows,
stained-glass doors and all. Again he's sitting at the top
of the stairs, this time wearing my hat. "In this light," I say,
"I don't recognize you." "You're the only person I won't kill,"
he says. I know he's thinking of telling me something more,
but won't. He starts to come down the stairs. "We all cease
to exist as persons. Solitude alone can make love possible,"
I say. "Paz," he says. "Good luck with that."

UNDER THE VOLCANO

The funeral passes by me sipping another mescale outside the café.
"Para todo mal," says the waiter. I'm skimming a novel about
a man who hid himself until he disappeared. I put it down and

take up *Another Mexico* inscribed on the fly leaf in pencil "To Brian.
Good luck with the book. Graham Greene." As I lay it down
a cloud swamps the sun. When it reappears it burns my books

which I take and shelter in my sack. Under pepper trees by Goya,
under the iron cross a magpie sits on, there are peppers and tomatoes
piled up on blankets, and more tomatoes like beating hearts. Drums

move shuffling girls down the hill. Who are they? You can know
too much. Behind me, two mongrels argue over a chicken foot and
behind them the city squats on centuries like a comic book drawing.

An old man is scooping up vivid weeds to fill out his bunch.
A fly, heavy, black and bright, keeps at me. Smoke stains the air
as a child is doing cartwheels under the volcano.

PROCESSION

Last night, in the smoke, the moon had a seizure, wobbling so
you couldn't understand it. Flowers on the hillsides are still confused,
flying off in the remaining wind while peasants are following

a funeral, heading for the horizon lost in blue lightning.
The dead man's feet point backward to the maize fields where
he was born. A dog gnaws a bone in the dirt. No sign of policia.

Later in the cafe, Ignazio the organizer tells me he'd read in an old book
about a fountain in the rocks where the water pours out and becomes green,
and about a turquoise spring that sings between pebbles and the bell-bird

responds. The song of the water, he says, sounds like tambourines.
"Where is this place?" I ask. "Nowhere," he says. "It's called Tonacatlalpan.
Only for princes, owners of the world, a world only for princes, nothing

for the common folk, those who suffer torment and misfortune here
on earth." Another procession passes, this time a wedding and the air
is suddenly clear as glass. I recall Ignazio's mother telling me that

Motecuhzoma had many mirrors in his palaces, so he was everywhere
and nowhere, exaggerated, diminished, getting lost in them, in himself,
and the mirrors broke, and he was scattered in little pieces.

HISTORY

"*Sangre y palabras*
Dejamos a nuestra hijos"
—Homero Aridjis

The craftsmen picked a feather carefully and placed it,
  from green birds, yellow birds, from jade brought out the jade,
from gold the gold, bejeweled the sun, wove the glow of brittle jade,
  from the flower brought out the flower, turned flayed skin to flowers
where now mothers sit in rebozos, babies at the breast, among
  child beggars, parrot-colored taxis, black armored vans, pink crosses
on black telephone poles until the wailing around midnight, the moon out
  in back streets where a veiled woman in white walks beside girls
who'd wept as priests cut their throats and laid their bodies in
  the lake's whirlpool that swirled the blood away with jewels, stones,
gold, before people in silence returned to the city with its rubble
  from the quake still in the streets where a young girl in a shawl sits
on the sidewalk selling lizards beside me on a bench reading *Poesia
  Indigena* where beings and things diffuse, beauty and blood fuse,
while over my head ripening fruits are light taken in and shaped to fit
  their own shadows falling over me with at my feet tranced flowers
yellow, red and white, mottled like the thighs of the divine mother
  who was painted with chalk and fed deer hearts, for whom men danced
in feathers then turned to deer that went to live on the high barren plain
  whose music is echoic so I can hear it over the hubbub, over the cathedral
that is a temple ransacked and remade, and I think of how we invent
  our selves and spread them out, before, behind, flayed thin, skins we
live in to dream. When I look up, there's a great bird, engulfed in sky,
  leaving marks to be read like back-fires or the after-images of flame.

MAQUILADORA

On the flat roof, three women
in startling white are combing

hair thick as sisal rope, one
after the other reaching

for an hibiscus to fix among
poppy, marigold, squash as

silver flares from black braids,
fish flash from waves, but

the perfume of maquiladora is
spreading, a whistle blows,

the women go and in their place
a sparrow, a starling, and a crow.

EL GRITO DE DOLORES

                              rings from the balcony of the National Palace,
beamed everywhere, the cry of Independence. *Ah,* cry the peasants,
let us leave these small plots, these ejidos, and head north, braving
coyotes, desert and thirst for the fields of California and the meat-packing
plants of Iowa, and *suck, suck* go the Indian babies at the breasts of their
barefooted mothers on Calle Cinco de Mayo and the flanged twig brooms
go *swish, swish* along the Calle Insurgentes, sweeping the library steps and
my gas-heater, my *calentador,* gets too hot for its own good and explodes
pop, pop like the wooden guns of Subcomandante Marcos rising out of
the Chiapas forests as in the National Palace Diego Rivera's mural of a
utopia waves bravely from its wall and peels and I am trying to read months'
notes on the meaning of sacrifice as the Grito de Dolores pours out of the radio
and "La Jornada" open on the table praises the Zapatistas and curses me and mine.

IN THE GARDEN OF THE HOTEL HUIZILOPOCHTLI

The Indian waiter turns to fire that flowers and
                    disappears into a monarch butterfly
making its way across the clatter of dishes into sunlight
                    prowling like a jaguar through the sunflowers,
under the calla lilies and bougainvilleas until a
                    brief shower brings quetzal flowers falling
on stunted savin junipers, and when it stops the fire-serpent
                    swallows it again, and the green jay's call vanishes into
the indigo mockingbird, into day's smoking mirrors,
                    and I forget who I am and vanish into
the still-beating heart of a chili-red flower near which hangs
                    Huitzilopochtli, arms and thighs blue, face crimson,
ready to plunge into the flower's heart his sharp
                    obsidian beak for new fire to take back to the sun,
over the broken bottles under the maguays, over
                    the motorcycle crash and taxi pile-up, over
the Mazahua beggar and old women down from
                    the hills with multi-colored fruit, past the codices
still burning in government offices, over the flag
                    of the republic toward Popocatepetl, across the lake
we float on, México-Tenochtitlan-Distrito-Federal.

ORIGIN MYTH

Florentine Codex, bk. 10, ch. 29

Good maguay they found that made good aguamiel.
His mother found it, Mayahuel. She also found firewater.
Johnny Walker, it was called, Dimple, Pinch, Cutty Sark.
Cuextecatl the tlatoani drank it. He wouldn't share.
He asked for more, and more, until he stood up, tore off
his breechcloth, took out his "divinity" and waved it about
like a prayer-stick so the elders expelled him and Mayahuel
and his whole family, so he drank a lot and never again
wore breech clouts, even in bed, just pyjama tops, no bottoms
so his divinity swung before him for all to see and they all
had to worship his divinity, and his wife became addicted
to enemas and netti pots and his daughter cut herself but
his son was afraid and for a present made up a box of songs
for his father. "Wake," said one, "the flames have risen.
Dawn is here. The flame-colored pheasant is calling, the flame-
colored swallow is flying and the flame butterfly is passing by."
But his father tore it open, then threw it across the floor.
"I thought it was a box of Montecristos," he said. And the son
in piety bled onto paper and burned it. But when his father
started to stick hairpins and knife-blades into his ears
and squeeze his nose red and pull out his eyelashes, when
his eyes turned puffy, teeth gray, wattles like a turkey,
the son made a polished mirror and held it to Cuextecatl's face.
But he knocked it aside and made his own mask of turquoise
snake teeth and quetzal feathers, and caught the train for the city,
promising never to return, but he did, again and again.

GHOSTS

Crossing the canal that led to the brackish lagoon, rain
stippling the surface a few marigold petals shivered on, a boat
came from the other side luminous as a monarch butterfly

while the festival behind lit fire after fire so the whole place
burned like an unhealed wound and as we passed we said nothing
for he was out of the pages of a book forever being written and I

his son, his washed-out palimpsest, a specter too, both making
the crossing as silhouettes, older than the surrounding mountains,
calm as if we didn't know each other and as I turned around

to watch his back, the tracks in the water were frayed cords
of the phone on which he called me to tell me to go to hell which
is where I went and where I found him again.

FIRE CEREMONY

One man, yellow and red, tasseled hat, green skirt ringed with seashells,
flayed skin draped over him, the face way down his back, genitals round
his neck, leading the other, chalk-white, tipsy, shorn head under plumed

headdress, hand in hand, "father" and "son," captor and captive, both
the same age, and one will tear out the other's heart, and start a fire in
his chest and it will be beautiful, the world renewed, fresh fire in the blood,

carried everywhere to destroy the old, and the son will live in the Sun's retinue
as he flies down the steps to be gathered by the father, boiled and eaten with
squash flowers, finger-bones ringing like gourd rattles, head-nerve singing,

thighs planted firmly in the pot, a flower-tree, the flower, *ciucatl*, the song,
xochitl, flowers everywhere, delicious flowers, palms, hip bones, ribs, forearms,
soles of the feet, select parts for the gods and select friends, torches to light

the world and the sun itself, fathers and sons illuminated from within where
everything is at stake, father and son united the way God before the beginning
of things used Himself as light, even before he said "Let there be light."

YOU COULD BE

                              inside yourself, salt in water, still to precipitate out.
You could be in a missing persons bureau not knowing where you are,
or in snow with no trace to follow, just dints the wind made. Yet things
burn here with a patient lazy glow, as in a furnished room with a coin-fed
gas fire where you glimpse yourself from time to time in the flickering
on the dusty furniture or cold oilcloth. There are many rooms to move through
where disembodied body might brush body. God's here too, somewhere,
concise as an almond, cool as the coils of hippocampus. His skin, chromium
as an early 60's Buick, flashes and fades as He goes to work digging a great
hole for what could eventually be more sky. He mutters and quotes Himself
a lot. There is no sun or moon, only a reasonable facsimiles thereof
made opulent by silence which is made of something we have no name for.
You know things here by feel, the body plenary as ellipses no paraphrase
can close. But for now that can be ignored. What works is what works,
and here you work as you try to get back out in front of yourself to become
for a while what you were before, clamber out of your reflection to become
literal again, though really, what's the point of that here among all these shards
and casques and caskabells, Tlaloc's flayed skins, Gargantuan shadows and
thread-like wings, blind rhyming things? It all holds together so you can count
yourself, all your incompletions, though you can never be complete here where
the world warps and the wrestler weeps and waves himself goodbye, and where
the economy is built on speculation that can go on forever, and need never crash
here where skies of satellites and stars talk to each other, to earthworms and coalseams,
celebrities and politicians on what seems an equal footing, and where there is
no design, no assigned circle, just patterns, the way we can't help connecting things,
dot to dot, note to note, as night sky mirrors thoughts and afterthoughts, fears
and hopes, and becomes stories, throwing back dark as a reflection of light that
was a reflection of dark, and so on, so we think we can see.

THE KNIFE

—Museo Nacional de Antropologia

Sleek as a mirror, still sharper than my new razor, it looks hungry just
lying there on its bed, *feed me, feed me*, the obsidian knife, the eternal child,
Tecpatl, son of Cihuacoatl, *Lady of the Snake Skirt* mother of all, who
opened her womb and dropped him from the sky and when he got lazy
she herself came and walked among the people dressed all in white with
him swaddled on her back until she left him in the market place where
a woman would find him crusted with gore and get the message and rush
him to the emperor who knew what needed to be done and soon the twin
staircases sang with repaid blood, the world righted and the skull-rack
swelled, and I keep looking through the glass at it, glass itself, through
my own reflected face to it, and when I get home I take from its dried-out
cardboard box my pocket-knife of best Sheffield steel with mother-of-pearl
handle, reclining unused on its brittle cottonwool bed, the only thing
worth having my father ever gave me, and which his father had probably
given him, a fetish I take everywhere I go, to no end that I can see.

BEHIND THE SUN

A woman pokes about in the pile with a stick, turning over
a radio's entrails while her son sits and plays with the frayed edges
of his shawl. The day before, he saw an eagle land on the stinking
ash and refuse. The blind are driven here and picked up late. They are
attracted by the firelight that somehow gets through or reflects off
the windows of new high rises, reaching higher and fading, building upward
as if they know what's on the other side. I pick up some dry petals and
a twig as the sun begins to set over Montaña Humiante and its shrines
to the Virgin, Mujer Blanca, over the maguays and Indian villages,
their toasted beans and caged toucans, their silver that bruised everything
it touched. I look up at Chapultepec, which gave its porphyry to the statue
in the plaza with the broken hands. The wind evaporates on the full black braids
of whispering women. I could ask them where to find some flowers for
my room, huge flowers of the sun, the shield-flower, *chimalxochitl*,
beautiful fragrant flowers. But I might as well ask the green flash of
hummingbirds, the evanescence of the tiny *pajaro mosca*. As I approach,
the women move away through broken blue-green laurels and scrub
the color of llamas, kicking up dust and the odd sparrow, all that's left
of Cuauhtemoc and his men who at death turned to birds jewel-bright
and went behind the sun to live in its wide fields of flowers, forever.

TLATELOLCO

Rain for days as
small blue birds
spiral up the bald cypress,
red birds circle
down, and where
they mingle is
Now, with flute and
sistrum, back-beat of
huehuetl, here the
wind's songs meet
the musicians of the sun
and I sneak up, binoculars
and notebook in hand,
until my feet sink into
mud and a cloud
drops and the birds
fly off so light's
lost and dogs begin
to bell as if the world
is falling into the lake's
lamp-black where fibers
swarm and lightning sparks,
as the storm gropes about
and I drop my glasses
and book outside myself
when the city burned
and rain melted it back
to mud, and Cuautemoc,
"Falling Eagle," The Sun,
surrendered at Tlatelolco
and time ended in
"a painful birth", says
the plaque at the site.

THE FLOWER WORLD

In the sedges and reeds of Chalco is the house of the gods, where day
and night a thrush trills, shining, while the petaled water stretches out
among the flowers, and there the quetzal bird sings too as the intoxicating
flowers bend to the sound of tambourines in praise of the Sun, who is here
in an urn with a turquoise collar, while rain blooms among the shadows
and the transvestites dance in bird costumes among flowers which are
the hearts and flesh of the gods we feed, for everyone is in the hands of
the Ruler of Death, who opens corollas and dries them up even here on
this vacant lot where everything's ablaze and the fire of destruction digs
deeper, eating through itself to the rust under everything, here where the
sanguinary scents of flowers turn to the stifling smell of concrete in the heat,
where cars feed roads and move like mirrors in and out of each other in front
of the Dominican church slaves built, where roofs with flickering aerials
turn aside in a sky further off than usual, thin clouds forming and reforming
as I lean against the blackened silk-cotton tree in the Place of Rains, near the
bus station on August 13, my birthday, the day Cortés captured Cuautemoc
in his torn finery, beside the market where headless things hang and flies hum
loud as the hummingbirds that move from one bright corpse to the other,
mistaking them for flowers and where fruits are carefully piled in pyramids on
which sit, here and there, butterflies opening and closing their wings like sails
and I recall on my way to school each gray morning stopping to gaze at the
incongruous glass door stained like a church window, from which a Spanish galleon
rose with billowing scarlet sails on cobalt waves out into the back lanes, over wet
cobbles toward the Tyne, past the Swan Hunter ship-yard, out to the North Sea.

NOTES

"Waves": see Daniel Defoe, *Tour Through the Whole Island of Great Britain*, vol. III, (1724-27).

"Places of Power": "various odds and ends of iron things" is from D.H.Lawrence, *Mornings in Mexico*.

"The Moon": "uccisi dai barbari tedeschi" = "killed by the German barbarians."

"Seabird": "con gli angeli" = "with the angels."

"El Grito de Dolores": This was the battlecry of the War of Independence, uttered on September 6, 1810, by Miguel Hidalgo y Costilla, a priest in the town of Dolores.

"In the Garden of the Hotel Huitzilipochtli": Huitzilipochtli, "Hummingbird on the Left / Southern Hummingbird", was the Mexica / Aztec god of the sun and warfare, creator god of fertility and patron deity.

"Fire Ceremony": "fire in his chest" = when a 52 year cycle was complete and the Pleiades rose to bring in the first day of the new calendar, a high-ranking captive was sacrificed on today's Cerro de la Estrella at a New Fire ceremony in which fire was made in the victim's chest cavity by fireboard and drill. From it a bonfire was lit and the fire carried throughout the city. The last ceremony was held in 1509, so our current cycle will end in 2027.

"History":"flayed thin, skins to live and dream in" refers to the ceremony of Tlacaxipehualitzli, "The Flaying of Men," "those who had been sacrificed were flayed and the Tototectin [Totec impersonators] put on the skins and wore them... and went from home to home," Diego Durán, *The History of the Indies and New Spain,* c. 1521.

"Origin Myth": "tlatoani" = ruler/king/emperor (literally "speaker").

"Tlatelolco": "huehuetl" = two-note drum. Cuautemoc was the last Aztec emperor.

ACKNOWLEDGMENTS

Some of the poems in this collection have appeared sometimes with different titles and in different versions in the following journals:

Agni: Taking the Sun in a Car-park beside the East River.
Boulevard: This House.
Cortland Review: The Ant.
Hotel Amerika: Under the Volcano.
Iowa Review: Coyote.
Kenyon Review: Salt, The Snake.
Miramar Poetry Journal: Heading Out, Becoming.
Missouri Review: Behind the Sun, The Procession, The Swan.
New Letters: The Flower World, The Fountain, The Visit.
North American Review: My Friend the Old Sailor.
Notre Dame Review: The Palermo Road, What Gives, Quantum for Breakfast.
Paris Review: Restoration of a Copy of an Imaginary Painting.
Plume Poetry: At Segesta, Limoni, La Viglia di Natale, Santa Maria in Trastevere.
Poetry: Time of the Fieldmice.
Prairie Schooner: The Breaks, Explorers, You Could Drive All the Way to Alaska, To a Mockingbird.
Salmagundi: Essay in Time.
Sewanee Review: The Gumshoe.
Southwest Review: The Flower World.
Stand (GB): The Smoking Mirror, Ghosts, In Xochiquetzal's Garden, Places of Power, The Thrush, Time's Scents.
The Journal: Breakdown.
The Plume Anthology of Poetry, 4: To Be Tree, Wall.
Warwick Review (GB): Fire Ceremony.